Dropbox for Business and Everyday Life

The Ultimate Dropbox Essentials Guide

Table of Contents

Introduction 6
Chapter 1: Understanding Dropbox for Business 7
   Features of Dropbox for Business 7
      Selective Sync 8
      Connect All Dropbox Accounts 8
      Remote Wipe 8
   How to Share In Dropbox 9
Chapter 2: Getting Started With Dropbox for Business 12
   Installing the App 12
      Installing the Desktop App 13
      Installing the Mobile App 14
   To Create and Manage Groups 14
      How to Create Groups 15
      How to Add Members to a Group 16
   Sharing Links and Folders 17
      Sharing Folders 17
      Sharing Links 19
   Connecting Your Dropboxes 19
   Managing a Dropbox Account 20

Admin Dashboard Overview 20

Remote Wipe Overview 22

Dropbox Badge..22

Chapter 3: More Dropbox for Business Tips 24

Dropbox Synching Icons 24

How to Move Files between Dropbox Accounts....25

How to Save Space on Your Hard Drive 26

Uploading Photos in Dropbox for Business............28

Two-Step Verification on Dropbox..........................29

How to Set Up the Two-Step Verification 30

How Will Two-Step Verification Affect Your Team 31

How to Reset the Two-Step Verification for a Team Member..31

Dropbox FAQs 32

Conclusion..35

Introduction

Today, people can take advantage of the many programs to manage their tasks and files so that they will become more efficient in the office. One such program is Dropbox which is a file-hosting service that provides file synchronization and cloud storage. With Dropbox, people can make a special folder in their computers which Dropbox can then synchronize so that it can be accessed whichever computer is used to view it.

Dropbox is a nifty program that you can use to make it easier for you to share files with other people. If you are still new with this program but you want to take advantage of it, then this book will serve as your guide as you navigate yourself with this program.

Chapter 1: Understanding Dropbox for Business

Dropbox for Business is a paid service that is targeted for the use of organizations. It provides administrative control as well as auditing for the IT departments while still allowing the users to create different cloud containers to separate work and personal documents.

The security features of the Dropbox for Business is high as it allows restrictions on sharing in order to limit the disclosure of confidential files. Moreover, users are also provided with different passwords for both personal and business accounts in order to control the access of the files unintentionally. This chapter will discuss about what you need to know about Dropbox for Business.

Features of Dropbox for Business

Dropbox for Business can help IT administrators make new integrations with other third-party technologies to build a tool to manage analytics, backups and content safety. Below are the three major features of Dropbox for Business that you should know about.

Selective Sync

The thing is that your computer has many storage spaces and this feature allows you to choose which folders you want to be synchronized with your computer and which ones you want to be stored online. This allows you to have access to your data from the Dropbox's website whenever you need your files. Moreover, it also allows you to have more storage space in your hard drive.

Connect All Dropbox Accounts

If you already have a personal account of Dropbox account, you can connect it to a work account without having to log on to each accounts. This means that you can jump between your vacation photos and your work presentations in just one click. Although you are syncing both accounts, they will still remain separate even if you can access them in one device.

Remote Wipe

Dropbox for Business can be accessed on any device from desktop computers, smart phones or tablet computers. If you lose any of your device which you use to access your Dropbox account, the last thing that you want to worry is the confidential files falling into the hands of the wrong person. One of the best features of Dropbox for Business is the Remote Wipe which allows you to delete the Dropbox folder from the linked device that you have lost. You can delete this by logging online to the other working devices that you have.

How to Share In Dropbox

All files start out as private files on Dropbox Business but you can still share all the files that you want. There are three ways to share files in Dropbox for Business and below are the ways on how you can do it.

- **Share a folder:** Sharing your Dropbox folder to collaborate with colleagues is very easy. In fact, you can share your Dropbox folder to anyone by default so that people can add, edit or even delete files inside your folder. However, if you are concerned about people making any unwanted changes in the file, you can set the *view-only permission* for all members of the folder. In the Dropbox for Business, you can choose to share links to people who are outside the folder.

- **Create a separate team folder:** If you want a universal folder where the entire members of your organization or department can access and edit, you can create a team folder. However, only the admin can create the team folders but once created, it can automatically be shared to everyone in the team so you don't have to invite all members of the team to check the folder. Team folders are also shared externally thus they are great for organization-wide documents such as training materials and work instructions.

- **Share a link:** Another way of sharing in Dropbox is to share links. By doing so, you can send copies of files like email attachment thus when you send others a link, they can easily view or even download a copy of the file but they do not have the ability to change your original copy. The best thing about Dropbox for Business is that you can send links even to people who do not have Dropbox. You also have the ability to control who can access the links and for how long by setting expiration and passwords for your link.

- **Send a file request:** If you want to collect files from multiple numbers of people, you can collect files from anyone and save the files in the Dropbox folder. The people who also want to get files from you do not need to get a Dropbox account in order to upload files to your file request.

Chapter 2: Getting Started With Dropbox for Business

Before you can use the Dropbox for Business, it is important that you install the desktop app so that you can create the Dropbox folder which will be synced to all your devices. This chapter will help you how to get started with Dropbox for Business.

Installing the App

Installing the Dropbox for Business app requires an invitation from your IT administrator. Once you get the invitation, you need to follow the instruction and fill your name as well as your password to create an account. Once you have a work account, you can then set up your personal account. It is important to take note that you need a separate email for your personal account so that your admin cannot access it. Once you have set up the password, you can start setting up by installing the app. Now, if you already have a Dropbox account, you will receive an email invite to join your team's Dropbox. This section will discuss the steps on how to install the app for both desktop and mobile devices.

Installing the Desktop App

First things first, install the desktop app because it lets you access all of the important files from your computer as well as those created from other mobile devices. When installing the Dropbox for Business app for the first time, your computer automatically creates a special folder dubbed as the default Dropbox folder. The folder has unique properties that update your files so that they remain the same when accessed using other devices. Installing the desktop app is very easy and below is the steps that you need to follow to be able to successfully run it on your computer.

- Download the installer by going to the site's page.
- Open the file and double click to start installation.
- Once the installation is completed, log in to your account. This should have been provided by your admin.

As soon as your desktop application is installed, you start sharing files on the Dropbox folder. You can do this by clicking the small blue icon on the system tray.

Installing the Mobile App

The best thing about Dropbox for Business is that you can access it from your mobile devices. However, before you can access your files from either your smart phone or tablet, you need to install the mobile app. The mobile app can support iOS, Windows Phone, Android and Windows tablet. If you are going to download the mobile app, make sure that you download the one that is compatible with your device. Once you have installed the mobile app, sign in to your Dropbox account using your email and password.

To Create and Manage Groups

Groups are a great way of managing Dropbox for Business teams thus making it easy for each member to collaborate with one another. By creating groups, you can create as well as manage lists of members to share different types of information directly with one another. This saves time instead of adding each person to the Dropbox individually.

Any member that you add to the group can automatically add them to the shared folders of the group. The thing is that groups can help teams manage their access to the shared folders. You can also make a list of people that can have access to the files and folders. So how do you create and manage groups? This section will discuss what you need to know about creating and managing groups.

How to Create Groups

Creating a group is fairly easy. Below are the steps on how to create a group on Dropbox for Business so that you can start sharing folders and files.

- Create a group; you need to sign in to your Dropbox for Business account.
- On the left sidebar, click on the tab that says **Sharing.**
- Look for the **Groups** tab and click on it.
- Click on the **Create group** button which is located at the upper right corner of the page.
- Type in the name of your group on the blank field. The group name will be the name that all team members will see to be able to see the shared folders. As the owner of the group, you have the ability to change the name of your group at any time.
- Click the **Create group** button.

Now if you don't see the **Create group** button, the only reason for this is that the team admin of your

Dropbox for Business may have restricted your team's ability to make the groups.

How to Add Members to a Group

If you are the owner of the group, you can add as well as remove members. It is important to take note that only members of the Dropbox for Business team can be invited into the group that you have created. This means that only those that belong in your organization can be invited to your group. Moreover, adding team members to a group will trigger different invites to each folder available to the group. To add a new group member, you can do the following:

- Sign in to your account.
- Click on the **Sharing** tab which is located at the left sidebar of the page.
- Click on the **Groups** tab and choose the name of the group you want to add new members to.
- Click on the **Add members** button which is located at the upper right corner of the page.
- Enter the names of people whom you want to invite and click the **Add members** button.

Sharing Links and Folders

Sharing folder and files is essential in Dropbox for Business because it allows teams and members to collaborate. So rather than managing different versions of your file and emailing them back and forth to the other team members, you can save a lot of time and trouble if you share files instead. The best thing about sharing files on Dropbox for Business is that users have the option to decide if the other members can edit the files or just view them.

Sharing Folders

Sharing Folders from the Desktop

Sharing folders is a more common approach Dropbox users prefer especially if they want other people to collaborate. To share folders, you need to follow the following procedures below:

- Sign in your Dropbox for Business account
- Click on the rainbow folder icon which is located at the top and center portion of the screen.
- Choose the option **"I'd like to create and share a new folder."**

- Name the new folder.
- Enter the email address of the people that you want to invite and add a personal message to inform the team members that they can view the shared folder.
- Instead of using the email address of members, you can also enter the group name because it is an easier option to add members.
- Set permission and folder settings then click on the **Share folder** tab.

Sharing Folders On iPad or iPhone

Mobile apps allow you share files as well as folders even if you do not have any access to a computer. There are different ways of sharing folders using mobile devices. Below are the steps on how to share folders on your iPad or iPhone.

- Swipe left or right over the file or folder that you want to share to reveal a set of icons.
- Tap the sharing icon which shows an upward arrow that comes out of the box.
- Choose the way you want to share the link. You can share the link like email, text message or Facebook page.
- Fill out the information needed to post or send the link.

- Tap the sharing icon that looks like an upward arrow that comes out of a box.
- Select **invite to folder.**
- Fill the information that you need to send invitation.

Sharing Links

Aside from sharing files, you can also send links to team members and clients. You can link to either files or folders for convenience. The benefit of sending or sharing links is to let clients see the files even if they do not have any Dropbox accounts. This is a great method for broadcast sending than for collaboration because other people cannot edit the original file so it remains safe and intact.

Connecting Your Dropboxes

Connecting personal and business Dropboxes allows you to access all of your accounts from all your linked devices while still keeping data separate. If you have a personal account where you keep your photos and a business account where you keep client information and projects, Dropbox for Business can let you connect all accounts and access them easily.

Connecting both personal and work accounts on the Dropbox for Business website is the first step to convenience. Below are the steps on how to connect your personal and work accounts.

- Sign in to your business account.
- Click on your name located on the top right corner of the page to open the account menu.
- Choose the **Connect a personal Dropbox** option.
- Create a personal account or sign in if you already have an existing one.
- Confirm your settings.

Managing a Dropbox Account

Managing your Dropbox for Business account starts with the dashboard overview. This section will discuss about what you need to know about managing your Dropbox Account.

Admin Dashboard Overview

The admin dashboard serves as the user interface of the Dropbox for Business app. It is where you can see all the icons, buttons and basically everything that you need to be able to use the app effectively. It also provides an insight regarding your team's activities aside from the shortcuts and the usual admin actions. In order to see the dashboard, you need to sign in to your Dropbox account. Once you are there, click on the **Admin Console** tab which is located on the left side bar of the page to get to the **Dashboard.** The dashboard has many functions and below is the list of things that it can offer to all its users.

- **View crucial stats and data:** The data that you can see in your Dropbox dashboard include the current number of members you have, licenses and pending invites.
- **Find a particular team member:** You can easily locate a particular team member by searching for his or her name in the Dropbox database. This is especially true if you want to share a particular file or folder to a specific member.
- **Send reminders:** You can send anyone with pending invites to join your team.
- **Invite new members to the team:** Perhaps the greatest thing that the dashboard can do is that it can help you invite new members to join your team so that sharing files and folders will be easier.
- **View usage data:** You can see how much the team is using Dropbox and how much space is

left so that you can further manage your Dropbox account to make it more effective.

Remote Wipe Overview

Sine Dropbox for Business allows you to share files to other people within your team using not only desktop computers but also mobile devices, there is a possibility of losing your mobile devices with the information shared on your folder being seen by outsiders. What you can do is to take advantage of the Remote Wipe feature of this app wherein it allows you to delete Dropbox folder from the device that you have lost from the Dropbox's website.

Once you unlike the device and choose this option, the device will automatically stop synchronizing all your devices as well as the Dropbox folder. Moreover, the app will continuously attempt to delete the folder whenever the device is online.

Dropbox Badge

The Dropbox badge allows you to collaborate with other desktop apps such as Microsoft Office tools among many others. With this feature, you will be able to do the following:

- **Update the file to its latest version:** If a member saves a new version of the file that you are working on simultaneously, the Dropbox badge will help you to automatically update the file to the member's latest version.
- **Check that is checking or editing the file:** The Dropbox badge shows the initial of the members or users that are viewing or even editing the file that you have opened. This is a great feature because it avoids people from creating different versions of the file.
- **Ask for feedback on a particular file:** You can click on the **Comment** button to encourage other users to create a feedback or contribute new contents to the file.
- **View file history to check the changed or deleted contents:** This feature also allows you to see the changes made on a particular file. You can do this by clicking on **View File History.**

It is important to take note that the Dropbox badge works well with Microsoft office tools, but it can also support the 2011 Office files from Mac operating systems.

Chapter 3: More Dropbox for Business Tips

Sharing files and folders with Dropbox for Business is relatively easy but there is more to this app than just sharing files. Thus, this chapter will discuss more tips to make it more convenient for you to use Dropbox for Business.

Dropbox Synching Icons

As soon as you finish installing the app, you can start saving all files that you want on the Dropbox folder. It is important to take note that the Dropbox folder works just like your ordinary computer folder. This means that if you want to save a particular file to this particular folder, all you need to do is to drag and drop.

Aside from saving the files on Dropbox for Business, it is important that you know to sync icons on your Dropbox to save time on your files. This section will discuss about the different syncing icons that you need to know about Dropbox.

- **Green check:** This refers to all files that are saved on your website and are accessible from any types of devices.
- **Blue arrows:** This refers to the files that are on the process of being saved on your website as well as other devices. However, the time that they get saved on your Dropbox folder depends on the internet connection, number and size of files can affect the amount of time your files need to be saved on your folder.
- **Red X:** Refers to files that are not working properly such as files not being synced properly. In most cases, the problem will correct itself but if does not correct itself, you can contact the administrator.

How to Move Files between Dropbox Accounts

You can move files between your personal and work Dropbox accounts. Just like transferring folders from your computer, you can move files from your Dropbox accounts is as easy and dragging items from one account and dropping it on the other.

However, it is important to take note that the owner of the folder or the admin can set restrictions on sharing and if you still continue to share files and folders despite the restrictions, you might end up with a non-shared copy that does not synchronize with the changes of the files seen by the other members.

How to Save Space on Your Hard Drive

When you save files in Dropbox, they will usually take up some space in your hard drives just like any regular files do. This can be bothersome especially if you have limited space in your hard drive. Now if you delete your files from your Dropbox folder, what happens is that you end up deleting the files from the other devices that are connected to the Dropbox folder.

Fortunately, Dropbox for Business can help you save space in your hard drive by using the Selective Sync feature. What this feature does is that it allows you to choose only the folders that you want to be synchronized to your computer so that you only have the files that you need saved on your computer. This section will discuss what you need to know about how to save space on your hard drive using the Selective Sync feature.

Using the Selective Sync feature is very important especially if you are sharing a lot of files and folders from your Dropbox for Business account. Below are the steps on how to use this feature to save space on your hard drive.

- Look for the **Dropbox icon** located on the system tray and click on it.
- Choose on the **gear icon** and choose **Preference** from the menu.
- Look for the **Account** tab and click on it.
- Choose the **Selective sync** button and click on it.

Once you are done, a window will appear which contains a list of all the folders inside your Dropbox folder. The folders that come with a check next to them will be automatically synchronized to your computer. You can uncheck any folders that you do not need to save on your hard drive. Click **OK** once you are finished. The folders that are not selected will be eventually removed from the hard drive but will still be available on the computer. You will know that the folders have been synced if they display a green checkmark which indicates that they have been completely uploaded on your Dropbox account.

Uploading Photos in Dropbox for Business

Dropbox for Business does not only allow you to share files and folders but also photos. This app comes with nifty camera features. This section will discuss about the different camera features that you can use on Dropbox.

- **Camera upload:** This feature is available for all desktop and mobile devices. While it was originally available only for the personal Dropbox accounts, this feature became mainstay for the business account since 2014. With this feature, automatically saves the photos that you take to a folder in your Dropbox account. This saves a lot of time and effort of uploading individual photos to your account. However, this feature does not provide control about what specific photos can be uploaded and organized to respective folders. Reviewing and organizing it to your folders or accounts are entirely your responsibility.

- **Photos page:** The photos page on the Dropbox website shows photos from your personal folder while the photos page of is accessible in another link. Separating your personal and work photos protects your privacy.

- **Screenshots:** Once you can connect all your Dropbox accounts, you can take screenshots from your computer and it will be automatically saved to either your personal or work Dropbox account depending on where you intend the screenshots to be. In any case, you will be prompted which account you want the images to be saved the first time you take a screenshot.

- **Albums:** Should you decide to move photos between your works to your personal Dropbox account, you can do it easily through drag and drop. However, if you want to move the entire album, you will not be able to do this. Moreover, it is important that you can only do this on your desktop device.

Two-Step Verification on Dropbox

The two-step verification is an extremely important security feature that adds another layer of protection to your Dropbox account. This means that your Dropbox account will require a six-digit security code aside from the conventional password once you sign in. This security feature is very important especially if you have highly sensitive files saved on your Dropbox folder. This section will discuss what you need to know about the two-step verification for Dropbox.

How to Set Up the Two-Step Verification

It is important to take note that team members will not be protected by the two-step verification until they have already set it up. Below are the steps on how to set up the two-step verification.

- Sign in to your account.
- Open the **Admin Console** and click on **Authentication.**
- Click on the **require two-step verification** tab and start assigning a confidential six-digit password for your account.
- Choose if you require two-step verification for selected team members or everyone.
- If you choose **require for specific members,** type in the email addresses of the team members then click the **Proceed** button.
- The two-step verification will become active and the two-step verification will appear on the **Authentication** page.

How Will Two-Step Verification Affect Your Team

When you require the two-step verification to your team, all individuals who will be invited in the future will be required to activate their two-step verification. It is important to take note that requiring such verification will not interrupt the workflow of the team members in any other way. What it does is that it just makes their Dropbox folders and files more secure against hackers and outsiders.

How to Reset the Two-Step Verification for a Team Member

In most cases, there will be team members who will forget their two-step verification password or even lose their device. If this happens, it is important that you know how to reset their two-step verification so that they can create a new one. Below are the steps on how to reset the verification password from their Dropbox accounts.

- Click on the **Admin console** and click on the **members** tab.
- Look for the name of the team member who wants his or her password reset.

- Once you have located the name, clock the gear icon that is next to the member's name.
- Click the **Reset two-step verification**.
- Once done resetting, the team member can then assign a new verification password.

Dropbox FAQs

Dropbox for Business is a relatively simple and straightforward app that any businesses can be used Below are the frequently asked questions (FAQs) that you need to know about Dropbox for Business.

- *Can I still sync if my hard drives do not have enough space?* When you save a file to your Dropbox account, it takes up space on your computer hard drive. This can eventually cause problems especially if your hard drive does not have a lot of space to sync to your Dropbox. Clear some files first before you start synchronizing.

- *How does this feature work with shared folders?* If you are a team member and you have an account to Dropbox for Business, you can share folders and sync them together. If the folder is too large for your hard drive, you don't need to delete files to share synced folders on your Dropbox account.

- *Can I delete from a shared folder without affecting the shared folders of the members?* Deleting files from a shared folder will not affect everyone else's workflow if you use the Selective Sync feature. In fact, if you remove the entire folder, the entire shared folder will be removed only from your account and not from everyone else's Dropbox.

- *How can I add licenses on my Dropbox account?* There are hundreds of licenses that you can add to your Dropbox for Business account. You can add licenses by going to the Admin Console of your account page. You can also quickly add licenses from the dashboard by clicking the **Remaining licenses** tab to get to the **Add license** option.

- *Can the number of files affect the performance of my Dropbox for Business account?* The optimal performance of the Dropbox for Business app relies partly on the number of files that you have. In fact, the app can once you have more than 300,000 files. This soft limit of amount of files also depends largely on the hardware specs of the computer that is running the Dropbox application. This means that there are some users who do not find issues despite that they have more files than the recommended soft limit. But as a general rule, it is recommended to have more than 1 million files on a single computer.

Conclusion

Sharing files and folders have never been so easy with Dropbox for Business. This is a file-sharing app that allows you to share files, folders and even links to other users. It is geared towards improving the data and document sharing of companies. With this app, it is very easy for everyone in the team or organization to access files that are needed in a prompt and secure manner. The Dropbox has great features to offer to its many users and if you haven't used this app yet then now is the time for you to install this app and enjoy its benefits.

Copyright © 2015. All rights reserved.

Except as permitted under the United States Copyright Act of 1976, reproduction or utilization of this work in any form or by any electronic, mechanical, or other means, now known or hereafter invented, including xerography, photocopying, and recording, and in any information storage and retrieval system, is forbidden without written permission.

The ideas, concepts, and opinions expressed in this book are intended to be used for educational and reference purposes only. Author and publisher claim no responsibility to any person or entity for any liability, loss, or damage caused or alleged to be caused directly or indirectly as a result of the use, application, or interpretation of the material in this book.

Printed in Great Britain
by Amazon